Secrets
of Tut's Tomb
and the
Pyramids

by
Stephanie Ann Reiff

A

Book

From

RAINTREE CHILDRENS BOOKS
Milwaukee • Toronto • Melbourne • London

Copyright© 1977 by Contemporary Perspectives, Inc.
All rights reserved. No part of this book may be reproduced or utilized in any form
or by any means, electronic or mechanical, including photocopying, recording, or
by any information storage and retrieval system, without permission in writing from
the Distributor and the Publisher. Inquiries should be addressed to the
DISTRIBUTOR: Raintree Publishers Limited, 205 West Highland Avenue,
Milwaukee, Wisconsin 53203 and the PUBLISHER: Contemporary Perspectives,
Inc., Suite 6A, 230 East 48th Street, New York, New York 10017.

Library of Congress Number: 77-22770

Art and Photo Credits

Cover photo and photo on page 13, Camera Press/Photo Trends.
Photos on pages 7, 8, 10, 11, 15, 17, 23, 35, 38, and 45 Wide World Photos.
Photo on page 14, Eliot Elisofon, Life Magazine,© Time, Inc.
Illustrations on pages 19, 20, and 36, Isadore Seltzer.
Photos on pages 27, 28, 31, 32, and 40, The Metropolitan Museum of Art,
photographs by Harry Burton.
All photo research for this book was provided by Sherry Olan.
Every effort has been made to trace the ownership of all copyrighted material in
this book and to obtain permission for its use.

Library of Congress Cataloging in Publication Data

Reiff, Stephanie.
  Secrets of Tut's tomb and the pyramids.

  SUMMARY: Discusses the building of the Egyptian pyramids,
strange stories associated with them, and possible powers possessed
by pyramids.
  1. Pyramids—Juvenile literature. 2. Tutankhamen, King of
Egypt—Tomb—Juvenile literature. 3. Egypt—Antiquities—Juvenile
literature. [1. Pyramids. 2. Tutankhamen, King of Egypt—Tomb. 3.
Egypt—Antiquities] I. Title.
DT63.5.R44   932'.01   77-22770
ISBN 0-8172-1051-2 lib. bdg.

Manufactured in the United States of America.
ISBN 0-8172-1051-2

Contents

CHAPTER 1

The First Pyramids

Imagine lifting enough stone blocks to build a wall running from Los Angeles to New York City. Each giant stone block weighs 2 to 15 tons. It will take almost 2,500,000 of these blocks! Now, picture building this wall without one modern machine! You have no wheels, no pulleys, and no levers.

Does this sound impossible to you? Does it sound like science fiction? Are we talking about a job for the "bionic man" or "bionic woman"? We are not. The Egyptians built pyramids more than 4,000 years ago, using those 2,500,000 heavy, limestone blocks. As far as we know, they did not use a single machine to lift those blocks into place. Yet, some pyramids are as high as today's skyscrapers. How these giant wonders were built is one of the world's great unsolved mysteries.

Just west of the Nile River in Egypt stands the fantastic *Pyramid Hill*. This is the home of the mysterious pyramids. At the edge of the Hill sits the stone creature called the *Sphinx*. The Sphinx is a statue of a lion with a human head. It seems to guard the entrance to the Hill. What a grand sight!

It is said that the Sphinx knows all. But, we know very little about the Sphinx. Why it was built is a mystery. And why was it built this way—half-human, half-animal? Some think the Sphinx contains buried secrets. Others think the giant statue drives away evil spirits.

How were these giant pyramids made? They rested on a square base. Four smooth, sloping sides made up the outside walls. And they were perfect triangles! Each giant triangle reached hundreds of feet in the air. At the top they met to form a peak.

The greatest pyramid of all time was built by an Egyptian King named Khufu. Later, the Greeks named him *Cheops*. Today, his Great Pyramid is known as the *Tomb of Cheops*. This

The mysterious Sphinx silently stands guard.

The Great Pyramid stands with its smaller neighbors.

giant pyramid stands in Giza. It is surrounded by many smaller pyramids.

The Great Pyramid of Cheops is the oldest and largest pyramid in the whole world. The base of the pyramid covers 13 acres. That's about seven long city blocks! And it rises 480 feet in the air. That makes it about as tall as a 40-story building.

Did you know that these pyramids were built without the use of modern tools? Does this mean Egyptians had magical powers? Before we try to piece together the puzzle of the pyramids, let's learn about the Egyptians who built them.

The very first pyramid was built in 2700 B.C. It was the idea of a "builder-magician" named *Imhoptep,* who wanted to please the powerful King Joser. King Joser was very worried about what would happen to his body after he died. He wanted to be buried with all his jewels and other riches. His grave had to be in a very safe place. Joser didn't want anyone or anything to disturb his eternal rest. At that time the Egyptian kings were buried in rectangular stone and sand buildings called *mastabas.* Joser didn't think mastabas were very safe. Grave robbers could break in and steal the King's body and his treasures.

King Joser wanted his body to be safe from these fortune hunters. He asked Imhoptep to think of some way to stop grave robbers from getting to his body. After quite some time, Imhoptep thought of a great plan. He changed the rectangular mastaba into a *step pyramid.* He built stone steps on top of the mastaba. The step pyramid looked very much like a cake with several layers.

The body of King Joser was buried at the very bottom of the step pyramid. The burial place

4

was similar to the one in the mastaba. But, the door to the body was hidden in one of the steps. Imhoptep was sure the King's body could never be found. But, the plan did not work. Kings would need something much better than the step pyramid to keep their treasures safe after death.

Why was death so important to the Egyptians? Shouldn't *life* have been more important? In a way it was. The Egyptians believed they would live again after death. They called their new life the *afterlife*. It was said to be more

Like a cake, this Step Pyramid was built in layers.

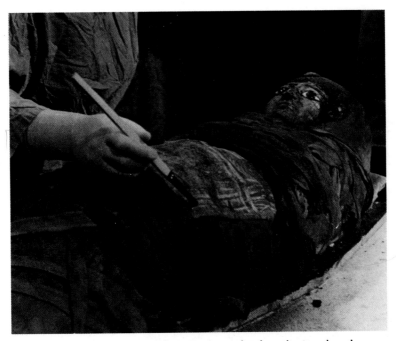

This is a mummy of a woman who has been dead
more than 2,000 years.

wonderful than life on earth. The kings made
many plans for their afterlife. They would make
sure it would be a happy one by taking their
treasures with them.

The king's body, too, had to be kept safe.
This was to help the soul, or spirit, return to the
body after death. The Egyptians believed that
within the body was a soul—a *ba*. They also believed that there was another spirit that joined
the body at death—a *ka*. When a person died, the
ka stayed on earth with the body.

11

It was very important for the body to be kept in good shape for the afterlife. The method they used to keep the body free from harm is called *mummification*. Preparing this *mummy* was not simple. First, the body was placed on a long, wooden table. The brain was destroyed with acid and then removed from the body. All of the other organs, except the heart, were taken from the body. They were placed in beautifully decorated jars. The king's priests were present for this strange ceremony. They chanted prayers and sang during each of the steps.

The next step was to clean the body. Then, to keep the body from decaying, it was rubbed with *resins*. (Resins are made from plants.) Then the body was wrapped with cloth. Finally, a very special prayer ended this process. This would help the body move and speak again in the after-life.

The king's body and the jar containing his organs were placed in the pyramid. So were the king's jewels, books, tools, dishes, games, and metals. Now, the king could certainly enjoy everything he loved in his first life. Life after death was so important that kings wrote books of instructions. They told what they wanted buried with them. They even listed people invited to the tomb!

This lid came from a jar containing a dead king's organs.

Imhoptep's pyramid for King Joser had a burial room and a temple. The King's instructions were followed well. All his treasures were buried with him. After the King died, the priests prayed for his return from death. But, even this giant pyramid did not keep King Joser's treasure safe from robbers! The step pyramid was just not good enough. Many pyramids were built in the following years. No one could build a better and safer pyramid. They tried different plans. They increased the size. Nothing worked until the Great Pyramid of King Cheops.

Nearly 2½ million huge stones were used to build the Great Pyramid.

The burial room was decorated to please the gods.

When the Great Pyramid of King Cheops was built, a clever builder found a way to make it more difficult for the robbers. This Great Pyramid had secret tunnels built into it. Cheops, a believer in magic, had built his Pyramid as a giant house of mystery.

CHAPTER 2

The Great Pyramid of Cheops

As many kings, Cheops was worried about his life after death and needed a safe burial place. It is said his Great Pyramid took 20 years to build. Over 100,000 men, women, and children spent part of their lives building the Great Pyramid. Each person spent three months a year working on it.

The cost of the Pyramid was huge, and the country fell into heavy debt. Thousands of workers died building Cheops' tomb. Even after his death, still more Egyptians died for the King. These people were killed by the priests to honor the Pyramid. Before dying, King Cheops ordered this to be done to please the gods of death. Another king gave his priests money to make sure

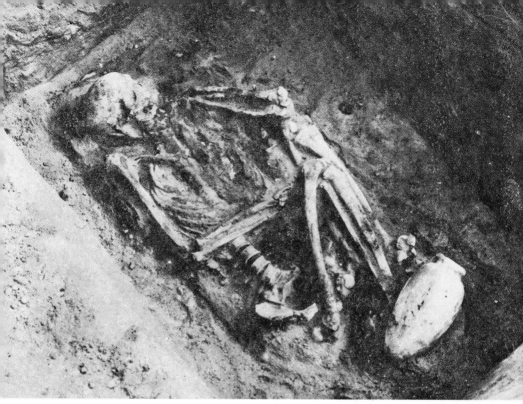
Here is a grave and the remains of a sacrificed worker.

that his soul returned to his body. The afterlife of the king was most important to him. He would try any plan that would give him his new life.

The Great Pyramid of Cheops stood 480 feet high. To build this huge tomb, many thousands of workers cut giant stone blocks. Each block had to be cut to fit in place. Workers carried these great, heavy blocks to the mouth of the Nile River. Some stones were taller than the people who had to move them. Then they were lifted onto rafts and boats and floated down the river. Finally, they reached the Valley of the Pyramids.

The trip to the Nile River was made through the deadly desert. Thousands of workers died from heat and thirst. How could they have lifted and moved those gigantic blocks across the desert? No one knows. Today, only their wood ramps survive. Not a sign has been found of even simple levers to lift the stones.

The building of the Great Pyramid occupied a great deal of the workers' daily lives. One expert on the pyramids believes that the people became more loyal to the Pyramid than to the King himself. More likely, the people of Egypt had no choice. They were bound to the King and his Pyramid.

The Great Pyramid was a giant maze. Long and short passages were built inside. Some walks and staircases led to rooms. Others did not. The ones that led nowhere were really traps for grave robbers. To move from room to room, one would have to go through many doors.

King Cheops was not buried at the bottom of the Great Pyramid. Instead, the King's workers built his burial room very high up, for safety. Some experts believe that King Cheops was afraid of being closed in. It is said that Cheops changed his mind many times about where he

Thousands worked for years to build the Great Pyramid.

should be buried. Each time, his burial room was placed higher in the Pyramid.

There were separate rooms for the King, Queen, and their family. There were also rooms for the priests and the treasures. In each room there were golden thrones, beautiful couches, and frightening statues. All the treasures of his life were buried with the King and his family.

The pyramids that were built after the Great Pyramid were not as large or lasting. This is because the kings of that period were not as impor-

Inside the Pyramid were rooms, passages, and traps.

tant as Cheops. These pyramids were not made of great, beautiful limestone, but of sand and stone. These later kings also worried about their souls returning to their bodies. To make sure the souls would safely return, they buried Pyramid Texts with them. These texts would keep away evil spirits that wanted to snatch them.

The sand and stone pyramids were not as strong as the stone pyramids, so only a few still stand today. There is one in Sakkara. It is the pyramid of King Unis. His pyramid has Pyramid Texts painted in blue on the white walls of his burial room. The writings were very important to the kings—as important as their treasures.

The texts, written on the burial room walls, are religious chants and mystical spells. They sometimes show us how a dead king will change into a star or even a human bird! When the king was not rich enough to bury a treasure, he would bury these writings. They would surely frighten away evil spirits for they had great magical powers. The texts would often picture the king as a mighty hero. Some appear to tell life stories of the king and his times.

During this time, stories were spread throughout Egypt about the "curse of the pyramid." Because of these stories, people believed that the Great Pyramid was haunted by evil spirits and deadly snakes. Even some grave robbers were frightened away!

It is exciting to think about how these giant buildings were made. We know the pyramids were formed from perfect triangles. But our history books tell us the *Greeks* invented geometry. How could these Egyptians, who built the pyramids 2,000 years earlier, have built perfect triangles without the use of geometry? Maybe our history books are wrong. Was geometry known in Egypt *before* Greece? The Egyptians also knew how to measure circles and squares. We know they were master builders, but were they also super scientists?

The Egyptians may very well have been astronomers. One scientist believes they invented the telescope, and that the Great Pyramid was used as a star observatory. One can read due North using the Pyramid as a compass. Were the Egyptians the first stargazers? Were they magicians? Before you laugh and say, "Of course not," remember something. We still don't know how they lifted those giant stones!

There are those who say that all of the 2,500,000 stones were lifted by magic. This magic

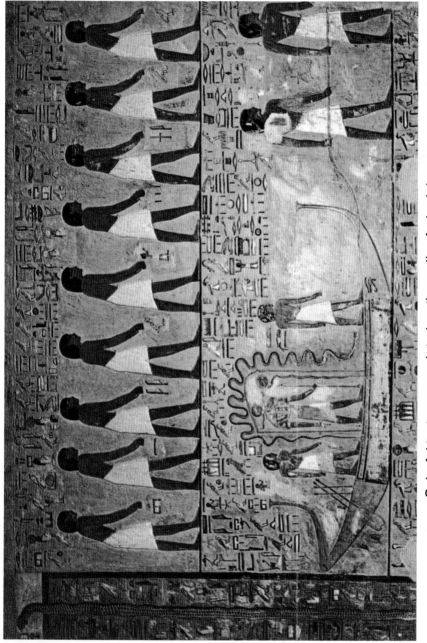

Colorful texts were painted on the walls of a burial room.

is called *levitation*. Believers in levitation think an object can be lifted by the powers of the mind. Some people who have studied the pyramids believe that the Egyptians raised those rocks by using levitation. Of course, there is no proof for this idea. But, if it were true, the Egyptians would surely be the world's greatest magicians!

The Great Pyramid is sometimes called a "bible in stone." Many people believe that an inch of the pyramid stands for a year of life. Some have even said that God built the pyramids! Is the pyramid a message from God? Is it really a stone bible? Maybe buried inside lie all the unsolved questions about life on earth. There are many people studying this idea today.

After almost 4,000 years, the Great Pyramid is still an unsolved mystery. Let's put together some of the clues. We do know that the Egyptians must have known science and mathematics. They must have known the length of the year. They knew the position of the sun at different times of the year. They plotted the direction of the North. They also had some idea of the weight of the earth. We think the Egyptians even knew the distance from the earth to the sun. Because of this, we may not be the first space explorers. Some people believe visitors from outer space taught the Egyptians.

In the next chapter we will join a team of scientists searching for some answers. It is a mystery story. The body of a king had been missing for thousands of years. The story of the search is a story of adventure, mysterious death, and strange, secret powers.

CHAPTER 3

Searching for the Tomb of Tut

The most exciting adventure story ever written is the search for the tomb of the "Boy King," known as *King Tut (Tutankhamen)*. History books were never the same after the searchers found the tomb. Neither were the searchers!

Our story begins in 1917 when two British adventurers made a trip to Egypt. They were Lord Carnarvon and Howard Carter. Both men had but one hope. They were searching for the tomb and the body of the great King Tut. Their adventure in the Valley of the Kings lasted over ten years. The two never dreamed what this trip would be like. Neither did the rest of the world.

In the fall of 1917, Carter and Carnarvon started digging near the Tomb of King Ramses VI. They dug for two years and found only old workers' huts. The work was long and hard. They dug for many more months and found nothing. Discouraged, they felt the Tomb of Tut would never be found. When almost all hope was lost, a clue was found. Carter discovered a doorway. It was hidden by a pile of rocks which took some time to clear away. But it was worth all the hard work. Carter found a royal seal on the door. He was sure that this royal seal belonged to Tutankhamen's Kingdom. What excitement at the end of the long, hot day! Now they were finally on the path to Tut.

The "Boy King" of Egypt was named Tutankhamen.

Carter (left) and Carnarvon (center) wrap statues.

Carter cut a small hole in the door. There were signs that someone had been there before. Grave robbers looking for gold pieces? Other explorers? Carter was very upset—someone had beaten him to Tut! But Carter had come too far to turn back now. What lay behind the door? Maybe nothing. Had earlier visitors seen something that would never again be found?

With the help of a candle, Carter peered inside one of the holes in the door. What he saw dazzled his eyes. A golden throne! The workers hurried to open the secret door completely. Inside, two black statues stood near the throne. There were beautiful vases and treasures the modern world had never seen! The two statues in the room faced each other. On their heads were giant cobra snakes. The statues looked as if they were guarding something. What was it?

Carter searched the room carefully. He found signs that others had already been there. Who else had come as far as he had? Where was the body of King Tut? Had it been stolen from the tomb? If so, the world would never know about the young King! This two-year search was near an end, but there would be no prize for all their hard work.

The room was searched and searched again. Carter was ready to leave when, suddenly, a shout was heard at the end of the room. One of the workers spotted another door! This one was built onto the wall, hidden between the two black statues. So that's what they were guarding! His mind was on fire! He walked to the wall to examine it closely. His heart sank. The door had fingerprints on it. Someone had been to this door too!

Carter wondered if he should call off the search and order everyone to go home. Just then, a worker cried out, "Another hole!" Carter rushed over to the worker's side. Sure enough, there was another hole. It was hidden under a beautiful couch.

Working their way through the hole, Carter's workers discovered an entrance to a small room. The room was filled with tools and beautiful painted boxes. It was so messy that it appeared the earlier visitors must have been robbers. How many objects were stolen? One robber had even left a scarf behind.

Now, Carter had his greatest disappointment. The Egyptian government suddenly called off the dig. Workers walled up all the entrances and many Egyptian guards stood at the tomb. Why didn't the Egyptians want Carter to go on with his search? Carter spent many weeks trying to begin his work again. If they could not continue, years of hope and work would be lost!

Carter pleaded with the Egyptian government. He explained how important this dig was to the world and to him. After several weeks he finally succeeded. The tomb was opened. Carter could go back to work. Every member of the team believed this dig would uncover the deepest secrets of the Egyptians.

People who dig through the mysteries of the past live only from moment to moment. They are always hoping the *next* chunk of rock will hold a clue. They go on digging for that one clue which may lead to yet another. They hope that all the clues will finally lead to an answer. And this was how it was with Carter and his team. They waited for the next big moment. When it finally came, it was fantastic!

This statue was found in the tomb of King Tut.

When Carter and the workers returned to the tomb, one worker discovered a large chariot! (It was a two-wheeled carriage probably pulled by horses. The Egyptians used such chariots for racing and in battles.) It took many long hours before the entire chariot was removed. In all, four huge chariots were finally found. They were too large to be lifted from the tomb. They had to be cut in half and put back together later in the museum in Cairo. stop

More searching, more clues, but Carter was still not satisfied. Where was the King's burial room? Where was King Tut? At that moment, Carter made up his mind. The hard work and

The chariots were found in Tut's Tomb.

long hours no longer mattered. He would not stop searching for Tut until each clue was retraced.

The whole team traced every step they had taken back to the doors, the room, the statues. Carter ordered the workers back to the doorway. Now he was able to cut a small hole in the door. When a light was flashed through, he saw a glorious gold door. Surely it was fit for a king! Were they close to the final resting place of Tut?

Carter was first to enter the room. Another world lay before his eyes. This room was painted with colorful pictures and strange letters. Were they messages to the gods? On the other side of the room Carter spotted another door. This one was locked. Forcing it open, he entered still another room. Looking about him, Carter was sure no man had been here since the death of King Tut. This was the "first" Carter was waiting for. No one had ever come this far. Not even robbers had been here. Carter could not hold back his excitement. Suddenly, he felt as if he were very close to King Tut.

It was later discovered that this was the King's family burial room. But, it was obvious that Tut, himself, had not been buried here. After searching the room, Carter discovered an open doorway that led to another room. Here, he found a chest covered with figures of four goddesses. The box held the organs of a human being. Could they be the King's?

But, once more, work stopped for a short time. Carter's partner, Lord Carnarvon, lay dying in a Cairo hotel room. His illness was a mystery to all the doctors called in to study his case. One doctor believed that he had been bitten by a poisonous mosquito. On April 6, 1923, Lord Carnarvon died. Most Egyptians did not believe that Carnarvon's illness was from a mosquito at all. They felt his death, and other strange happenings, were caused by the "secret powers" of the "Mummy's Curse."

Just before Carnarvon's death, most of the city of Cairo had a power failure. The Egyptian newspapers blamed the death of Lord Carnarvon and the power failure on the opening of Tut's Tomb. The papers called the power failure "an act of the angry gods." One headline read, "Death will come on swift pinions [wings] to those who disturb the rest of the *Pharaoh*" [a newer Egyptian term for "King"]. That very same message had been found by Carter. It was written on clay tablets in the tomb.

Even this did not stop Carter, who was not the least bit superstitious. In 1926, a determined

A solid gold chest held King Tut's organs.

Carter opened the door to Tut's holy room. Many of his workers were afraid of the "Pharoah's Curse"—but Carter still continued the search.

Once back inside the holy room, Carter and his team found not one, but *four*, coffins. Each one was opened separately. It took almost three months to complete this task. In the very last coffin, Carter found a splendid gold mask covering what seemed to be a head and shoulders. The face drawn on the mask was very young and handsome. Carter knew that King Tutankhamen died when he was still very young. Had he finally found Tut? Was this his coffin?

Removing the mask from the coffin was not easy. It was covered with a sticky material. Maybe this was the chemical used to help preserve the mummy. The workers peeled away the material stuck to the mask. Finally, lying under the mask, was the mummy of Tut. What a suspenseful moment! All in the burial room fell silent. Their years of hard work had been worthwhile, for the prize had finally come. Everyone wondered what would be uncovered next. Would the body of the young King still be preserved? Had it survived for centuries after his death?

Dr. Douglas Derry, another scientist at the site, carefully unwrapped the layers of cloth binding the body. Each layer of cloth was covered with gold jewelry. At last, the body was totally uncovered. Astonished, the scientists stared at the face and body. *Everyone knew at that moment they were gazing at the body of young King Tut.*

Much was learned about King Tut from pictures found in the room. He was pictured as a mean and harsh ruler. There were pictures showing him kicking people. Others showed him standing by while prisoners were being killed.

With all the clues put together, Dr. Derry learned two important things about King Tut's life. First, King Tut probably had died when he

A solid gold mask covered Tut's head and shoulders.

was only 18 years old and had ruled Egypt more than three thousand years ago. Second, iron was used by the Egyptians. Derry knew because this was the metal on the King's headrest.

Our history books have told us the *Greeks* were the first to use iron. If the Egyptians used iron, then they did have modern tools. Just think, people living almost four thousand years ago may have worked with tools similar to those we use today. A mystery which had puzzled the world for centuries was being solved in Tut's burial room.

The opening of King Tut's Tomb created great disagreements in Egypt. Some people were in favor of searching the tomb. Others were afraid the "Mummy's Curse" would now be let loose on the world. A statue in the burial room warned: "It is I who drive back the robbers of the tomb with the flames of the desert. I am the Protector of Tutankhamen's grave." Could this warning have been real? Read further and decide for yourself.

Twenty people were with Howard Carter in Tut's burial room. Within months after Tut's coffin was opened, 13 of the 20 had died. In almost every case, the death was due to an unknown cause. Lord Carnarvon's death was the first. Even his doctors could not explain it. The death of Arthur Mace was another. He was the scientist

Carter examines the coffin containing King Tut.

who helped Carter remove the parts of Tut's body. It was thought his death might have been caused by a germ living on the mummy. If so, this virus was able to live for 4,000 years. The doctors called it "coffin disease."

Perhaps the tomb *was* a mysterious and magical place where all living things survived. Even today, some think so. The secret powers of the pyramids deserve more thought. Let's try to uncover what is fact and what is fiction. Remember—not *everything* can be explained. There may still be powers unknown to man.

CHAPTER 4

The Secret Powers of Pyramids

Do the pyramids have special powers? There are people who claim the pyramids are magical. Many believe their shape can affect everything from plants, to pains, to personalities. Pyramid toys and games are being sold all over the world. People have placed small scale model pyramids under their beds and in sports locker rooms. A few dentists have even used them on their patients. Those examples are only a few of the ways modern people are testing the "secret powers" of the age-old pyramids. For many years, people have looked to the pyramids as the greatest fortune-tellers of all.

In the early 1800s, the Great Pyramid was thought to be a message in stone to the world.

Many years later, pyramid believers made the following predictions based upon the messages of the Pyramid:

- a great war would break out in 1928
- Christ would return to earth in 1936
- the world would end in 1953
- a magical number system would be revealed to the world
- the secret of living forever would be told
- people from other planets would show themselves to man

As far as we know, none of these things has come true. But, many modern stories point to hidden powers in the pyramids. Let's take a look at some of them.

If small pyramid models are built to the scale of the Great Pyramid of Cheops, plants placed inside are said to grow faster and healthier. If water is placed inside the pyramid, some say it becomes sweeter. It has also been said this water can be used to grow sweeter fruits.

Even more astonishing is that cuts, wounds, and burns have been reported to heal faster and are less painful if wrapped in a small pyramid. Some have reported that toothaches and tooth decay are lessened if placed under, or in, a pyramid. Dr. Garefis, one such believing dentist, has used pyramids in his work. He had pyramids hanging from the ceiling of his California office. They were hung just over the patient's head. Dr. Garefis believes that his patients had less pain and fewer cavities because of the powers of the pyramids.

Some say that razor blades, when placed in a small pyramid, remain sharp longer. Most recently, tests of "pyramid powers" were still being carried on at Stanford University in California.

Is it true that if a man or woman sleeps under a pyramid he or she will become smarter? One young couple did try to see if this was so. They traveled to the Great Pyramid of Cheops and decided to stay the night. They reported feeling suffocated while in the burial room. Many colored lights appeared before their eyes. As the night crept on, the young man felt as if his body were charged with strange energy. He then felt as if his mind were trying to leave his body. After this terrifying experience, the young man said that he felt as if he knew everything there was to know about the world.

CHAPTER 5

Strange Stories of Kings, Princes, and Pyramids

How the Sphinx Got Its "Dog Collar"

The Sphinx was built in front of the Great Pyramid in a hollow pit in the Valley of the Pyramids. Because it was built in a hollow, the desert sand blew in around it. Over time, the sands buried the Sphinx, except for its head. Thothmes IV ordered the Sphinx dug out. But the pit soon filled up again with sand. In later years, some soldiers treated the Sphinx badly. They used it as a target for gun practice. Aiming their guns at its head, huge holes were blown into this great, beautiful human lion.

In 1400, a Muslim, in a religious rage, smashed the nose of the Sphinx. Over the years, the sands of the desert once again covered the giant statue. But, in 1926, a British scientist had

Smashed and battered, the Sphinx lives on.

the Sphinx dug out for the last time. He feared the Sphinx might lose its heavy head completely. Something was needed to hold the head tightly to the body. So, he had an iron collar made to fit around its neck and support the weight of the head. That's how the Sphinx got its dog collar!

The Mystery of the Bent Pyramid

Bent Pyramids were built after the step pyramids. They were built to protect the kings' bodies from earthquakes and decay. Something strange happened in a bent pyramid in ancient Memphis. It remains a great mystery to this day.

In 1839, while some workers were digging inside, something was happening to the air in the pyramid. It became so hot they had to stop working. Then, there seemed to be no air at all! They were near death because of a lack of oxygen. Suddenly, a strong, cold wind began to blow. It blew chilled air through the pyramid for two full days. The workers were able to continue digging.

No one knew what caused the cold wind. After the second day, the wind died out. As suddenly as it came, it left, and never returned. Scientists believe that the cold air came from hidden passages in the pyramid. No such passages have ever been found. The chilling air remains an unsolved mystery.

The Great Ship of King Cheops

One of the world's oldest known ships was built by King Cheops. It was 140 feet long with oars that were 26 feet long. He built it for two reasons. First, it would honor his great life on earth. Second, his body could be carried down the Nile on the ship when he died. Cheops was certain this would make his trip to the afterlife smooth.

After Cheops' death, the ship was taken apart. All of its 1,200 pieces were marked. A set of instructions was left to show how to put the ship together. Then the instructions and ship parts were buried in an airtight pit near the Great Pyramid. Years later, scientists put the ship together again. Today, you can view this very same ship in a museum in Cairo.

The Secret Strength of the Great Pyramid

In 813 A.D. Abdullah al-Mamun, Prince of Egypt, wanted a map of the earth and the stars drawn. This gift to the world would prove his great power. He called all the wise men in his kingdom to come forth and tell how it should be done. Their answer angered the Prince. They told him that such maps already existed. They were buried inside the Great Pyramid. Seven years later, the powerful Prince ordered a search of the Great Pyramid.

This search was very difficult. After many weeks, no entrance to the Great Pyramid could be found. Al-Mamun was so angry he ordered a hole made in its side. If there were no entrance, he would build one! All attempts failed. The Great Pyramid could not be opened.

Four centuries passed. The Great Pyramid remained untouched. Earthquakes destroyed much of northern Egypt. The Great Pyramid stood. Could nothing destroy it?

The Egyptian royalty looked upon the Pyramid with hatred. Earthquakes had ruined much of their land. The country was now poor and the powerful Pyramid reminded the Egyptians of their glorious past.

These royal families, whose ancestor had been Prince al-Mamun, decided to steal some of the treasures of the Great Pyramid. They began to strip away the richly decorated covering of the Pyramid. This stone was beautiful limestone. Over many years they removed 22 acres of limestone. Finally, the whole covering of the Great Pyramid was gone. From its limestone, new bridges and palaces were built.

And so, even stripped of its beautiful stone cover, the Great Pyramid survived. It overcame the forces of greedy kings and nature. Its riches outlasted the wealth of the nation that built it. Even kings had to turn to the Great Pyramid to restore some of the beauty of ancient Egypt. And to this very moment in history, no human fully understands the secrets of the Pyramid.